D0198515

LAUREL LEAF BOOKS

There probably isn't a baseball fan alive who hasn't questioned a manager's decision. In this book, you will do more than question a decision—you will *make* it. You'll have to make that lonely stroll to the mound when your pitcher is in trouble, fill in your lineup card, and send signals to your third-base coach.

The problems you face may not be easy to solve. In fact, there may not be a right or a wrong solution. Luck can make a bad move look great and a good move seem like a terrible blunder. But with a championship at stake, the pressure is on. If a decision pays off, it could turn the game in your favor. If it backfires, thousands of fans are going to demand an explanation.

NATE AASENG is the author of numerous sports biographies, as well as *You Are the Coach—Hockey, You Are the Coach—Football,* and *You Are the Coach—Basketball,* which are all available in Dell Laurel-Leaf editions. He lives in Eau Claire, Wisconsin, with his wife and two sons.

ALSO AVAILABLE IN LAUREL-LEAF BOOKS:

YOU ARE THE COACH—FOOTBALL, *Nate Aaseng*

YOU ARE THE COACH—BASKETBALL, *Nate Aaseng*

YOU ARE THE COACH—HOCKEY, *Nate Aaseng*

SECRETS OF THE SUPER ATHLETES—SOCCER, *John Devaney*

SECRETS OF THE SUPER ATHLETES—BASKETBALL, *David Fremon*

SECRETS OF THE SUPER ATHLETES—BASEBALL,
Abbot Neil Solomon

SECRETS OF THE SUPER ATHLETES—FOOTBALL,
Abbot Neil Solomon

PLAY TO LIVE, *Charles Veley*

THE AVENGING SPIRIT, *Edward P. Stevenson*

DEMON TREE, *Colin Daniel*

BASEBALL: YOU are the MANAGER

Nate Aaseng

LAUREL-LEAF BOOKS bring together under a single imprint outstanding works of fiction and nonfiction particularly suitable for young adult readers, both in and out of the classroom. Charles F. Reasoner, Professor Emeritus of Children's Literature and Reading, New York University, is consultant to this series.

Published by
Dell Publishing Co., Inc.
1 Dag Hammarskjold Plaza
New York, New York 10017

Copyright © 1983 by Lerner Publications Company

All rights reserved. International copyright secured. No part of this book may be reproduced in any form whatsoever without permission in writing from the publisher except for the inclusion of brief quotations in an acknowledged review. For information address Lerner Publications Company, Minneapolis, Minnesota.

Laurel-Leaf Library ® TM 766734, Dell Publishing Co., Inc.

ISBN: 0-440-99829-8

RL: 7.8

Reprinted by arrangement with Lerner Publications Company

Printed in the United States of America

First Laurel-Leaf printing—February 1984

To Mark Lerner, whose attention to detail has greatly improved the quality of these books

ACKNOWLEDGMENTS

Photo credits: pp. 26 (top), 29 (right), 31, 76, Baltimore Orioles; pp. 53 (second from right), 57 (top), Clifton Boutelle; pp. 9 (far right), 19 (bottom row), George Brace; p. 64, Cincinnati Reds; pp. 53 (right), 57 (bottom), Detroit Tigers; pp. 7, 9 (left and second from left), 11, 84, Los Angeles Dodgers; p. 53 (left), 55, Thomas Donoghue; p. 56, Jim McKnight; p. 87, Minnesota Twins; pp. 15, 19 (top row and center), 20, 65, 67, 68, National Baseball Hall of Fame and Museum; pp. 36, 39, 40, 41, 42, 46 (left), 51, 92, 95, 96, New York Yankees; pp. 29 (left), 74, 77, 78, Pittsburgh Pirates; pp. 46 (right), 49, San Francisco Giants; pp. 73, 99, United Press International; p. 26 (bottom), Jerry Wachter; pp. 8, 9 (second from right), 13, 25, 34-35, 45, 53 (second from left), 61, 62, 83, 91, 100, 101, 103, Wide World Photos, Inc.

CONTENTS

Become the Manager!

It's late in the game and a rally is under way. Team A sends a pinch hitter up to the plate. Team B responds by calling for a new relief pitcher. No sooner does the pitcher finish his warm-up tosses than Team A replaces the first pinch hitter with another one!

You've just seen two baseball managers at work. Three key strategies have unfolded before your eyes without a single pitch being thrown. This example shows the important role that a manager and his strategies play in the game of baseball.

Baseball managers not only have to make the right moves, they also have to know when to make them. Is it time for a new pitcher? Is this the right moment for a pinch hitter? Do you want offense or defense at a key position? When will you steal a base, bunt, or intentionally walk a rival batter? Who is hitting well on your team, and how long can you expect his luck to hold out?

There probably isn't a baseball fan alive who hasn't questioned a manager's decision. In this book, you will do more than question a decision—you will <u>make</u> it. You'll have to make that lonely stroll to the mound when your pitcher is in trouble, fill in your lineup card, and send in signals to your third base coach.

The problems you face may not be easy to solve. In fact, there may not be a right or a wrong solution. Luck can make a bad move look great and a good move seem like a terrible blunder. But with a championship at stake, the pressure is on. If a decision pays off, it could turn the game in your favor. If it backfires, thousands of fans are going to demand an explanation.

So see how it feels to be in the dugout with the responsibility of running a club on your shoulders. Try your luck as you match wits with baseball's most successful managers in these ten contests to determine the divisional, pennant, or Series champs.

1 Relief from a Disastrous Finish

Dodger Stadium

You are managing the Los Angeles Dodgers.

It's the ninth inning, and you're facing the San Francisco Giants. This game will determine which of you will win the 1962 National League pennant.

Many Dodger fans are after your scalp for letting the pennant contest last this long. With only seven games left to play in the season, your team led the San Francisco Giants by four games. Yet the Giants closed the gap and forced a three-game play-off for the league title. You lost the first game and won the second one, so now the pennant rests on the outcome of this final contest.

The Giants gave you a scare by scoring two runs in the second inning. In the sixth inning, though, your best hitter, Tommy Davis, evened things up with a home run. Your Dodgers then moved out to a 4-2 lead going into the ninth inning. You were confident of winning until you remembered that 11 years ago the Dodgers had led the Giants 4 to 2 in the ninth inning of a play-off game and lost!

Reliever Ed Roebuck was pitching well for you in previous innings. Unfortunately, he started off this inning by giving up a single to the Giants' Matty Alou. The next batter, Harvey Kuenn, reached first base on a fielder's choice, forcing Alou out at second. Roebuck then lost control. He gave up two straight walks, loading the bases. As your other relief pitchers warmed up quickly, Willie Mays singled and a run was scored.

It's clear that you must replace Roebuck. The score is now 4 to 3 in your favor, with the bases still loaded and one out. Which man do you bring in to pitch?

The year 1962 has been Ed Roebuck's best as a pro. He's won ten games, lost only one, and earned nine saves. But now, in the last inning of the last game of the season, Roebuck has finally run out of gas.

You have four good pitchers ready for action.

Ron Perranoski and Larry Sherry have been excellent in relief all season, while Stan Williams and Don Drysdale have had fine years as starters. Here are their statistics for the year:

| | Perranoski | Sherry | Williams | Drysdale |

	Games	Innings	Wins-Losses
Perranoski	70	107	6-6
Sherry	58	90	7-3
Williams	39	186	14-12
Drysdale	43	314	25-9

	ERA	Strikeouts	Walks
Perranoski	2.85	68	36
Sherry	3.20	71	44
Williams	4.46	108	96
Drysdale	2.83	232	78

Perranoski is the only left-hander in the group. Percentages have shown that it is usually easier for a right-handed pitcher to get a right-handed batter out and for a lefty to get a left-handed batter out. The next scheduled batter for the Giants is power hitter Orlando Cepeda, who bats right-handed. Next comes left-handed Ed Bailey, and following Bailey is Jim Davenport, another right-hander. Ron had moderate success as a reliever in game 2 of this series.

Perranoski is only in his second full season as a major leaguer, while Drysdale, Williams, and Sherry are all veterans. In the past, Sherry has held up well under pressure. He was especially noted for being the hero of the 1959 World Series, when he completely baffled the Chicago White Sox. But this season he has been replaced by Perranoski as your ace reliever. In the first game of this series, Sherry was hit hard by the Giants.

Since the Giants have a man on third with only one out, even a fly ball hit fairly deep into the outfield could allow a runner to score. Therefore you would like a reliever who could deliver a strikeout or a ground ball. With the bases loaded, you absolutely cannot afford to give up a walk.

Drysdale can pitch in relief, but he is also one of your best starters. You have been planning to save him for the first game of the World Series, assuming you will win this game. Williams pitched surprisingly well in yesterday's game, picking up the win in relief.

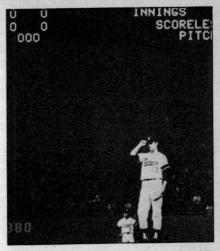

INNINGS
SCORELE[S]
PITC[H]

Big Don Drysdale's league-leading record in
1962 is as impressive as his size.

What's Your Decision?

You are the manager.
As you walk toward the mound you must signal
for the reliever to come in from the bullpen.
Who will it be?

#1 Perranoski
#2 Sherry
#3 Williams
#4 Drysdale

**Choose the pitcher. Then turn the page to find out
which pitcher the Dodgers' manager chose.**

The Dodgers decided to give the ball to Williams, #3.

That would set up a right-handed pitcher against a right-handed batter. Williams was a hard-throwing pitcher who could challenge Cepeda and the hitters that followed. The Dodgers were counting on him to continue his success against the Giants. With luck, he wouldn't have any of the control problems he was prone to. Being left-handed and fairly inexperienced, Perranoski (#1) was bypassed. Drysdale (#4) was being saved for the World Series start. Sherry (#2) seemed to be a risk since he had pitched so poorly in his last appearance.

Hoping for two strikeouts, Los Angeles brought in 6-foot, 5-inch, 230-pound Stan Williams to face the Giants. Could Stan's power pitching find the plate, or would his tendency to wildness bring down the Dodgers?

Here's What Happened!

Cepeda lofted a fly ball that sailed just deep enough to allow the runner on third to tag up and score the tying run. At the same time, the runner on second moved up to third. No one could really fault Williams at this point. At least the batter was out, making it two outs with runners on first and third.

But then Williams uncorked a wild pitch, allowing the runner on first to move up to second. Ed Bailey was intentionally walked, and the bases were loaded once again. The Dodgers continued to let Stan pitch to right-hander Davenport. The Giants' hitter decided to keep his bat on his shoulder and make Williams throw strikes. Williams could not find the strike zone, though, and Davenport walked, forcing in the lead run. Perranoski finally replaced Williams and finished the inning, but the damage had been done. Los Angeles lost the game 6 to 4 and handed the National League pennant to San Francisco.

The decision to go with Williams caused a lot of head-shaking in Los Angeles. Everyone knew Williams had control problems and that a walk would mean disaster. In addition, the plan to save Drysdale for another game while this contest was still in doubt struck many as a reckless gamble. By putting in either Perranoski or Drysdale, the Dodgers might at least have forced the Giants to earn their title with a hit, rather than giving it to them with a walk.

2 Too Early to Make a Move?

Celebrating their tenth straight win during the 1955 season are Dodgers (clockwise from left) Jackie Robinson, Joe Black, Duke Snider, Gil Hodges, manager Walt Alston, and Don Zimmer.

You are managing the Brooklyn Dodgers.

These are the lovable "Bums" who regularly win the National League pennant, only to be thrashed in the World Series by their crosstown rivals, the New York Yankees. This 1955 World Series may be your best chance yet to beat the Yankees. The Series is tied at three games apiece and you have a hot pitcher, Johnny Podres, working the final game for you.

The contest was scoreless until your Dodgers broke through in the fourth inning for a run off Yankee lefty Tommy Byrne. The game is now in the sixth inning. You have just scored another run and have forced Byrne out of the game. The bases are loaded, and you have a chance to build up a comfortable lead. Because there are already two outs against you, however, it will take a timely hit to gain that extra edge.

Due to bat next is second baseman Don Zimmer. After taking a long look at Zimmer and at the men sitting on the bench beside you, you have to decide if now is a good time to pinch hit and perhaps make some defensive changes.

You have three weak spots in your lineup.

No one on your team starts regularly at either second base, third base, or in left field. The legendary Jackie Robinson used to handle second base well, but as the years have gone by his legs have been slowing down. Although he still starts often, he is restricted to third base or left field.

Junior Gilliam and Don Zimmer now share the second base position. Gilliam is a good all-around ball player. When he is not at second base, he usually starts in left field. Whenever Gilliam plays second base, Sandy Amoros plays left field. In this game, you started with Gilliam in left, Zimmer at second, and Robinson at third.

If you pinch hit for Zimmer, Gilliam will take over at second and Amoros will move into left field. Amoros is a speedy, reliable defensive player who hasn't hit very well during the year.

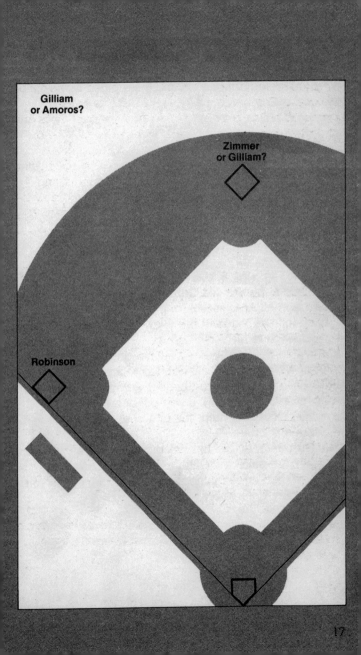

Gilliam
or Amoros?

Zimmer
or Gilliam?

Robinson

17

You have four possible pinch hitters for Zimmer.

When you compare the totals of these pinch hitters with Zimmer's, you find:

	Average	Home Runs
Zimmer	.239	15
Amoros	.247	10
Shuba	.275	1
Kellert	.325	4
Hoak	.240	5

Despite his poor average, Zimmer has shown some remarkable power. His total of 15 home runs in only 88 games ranks with some of the top sluggers on the team.

Frank Kellert, who had a fine season, has one hit in his three appearances in this Series. George Shuba, a veteran in his final season of play, produced 11 hits in 29 pinch-hit efforts during the year. He has not yet had a chance to hit in the Series.

You would prefer to have a left-handed batter to send up against New York's right-handed reliever Bob Grim. But Shuba and Amoros are the only two lefties among the five hitters mentioned. If you put one of them in the game, New York holds the option of switching to a left-handed pitcher.

Thinking defensively, you are probably better off with Amoros in left field and Gilliam at second base. But with more than three innings to go in the game, are you ready to play defensively so soon?

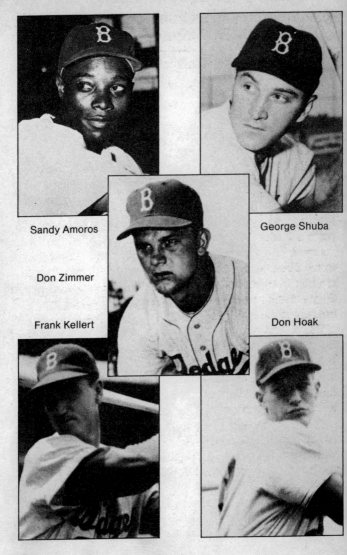

Sandy Amoros

George Shuba

Don Zimmer

Frank Kellert

Don Hoak

The Dodgers hope that young left-hander Johnny Podres' success against the Bronx Bombers can hold up through the seventh game.

A key factor here is how much confidence you have in your pitcher. Can he hold a two-run lead? In this Series, Johnny Podres has pitched far better than you had dreamed he could. During the year, he won only 9 games and lost 10, yet he has beaten the Yankees once in this championship series. In this game, he is continuing to give trouble to New York's hitters, who keep hitting under the ball, causing a lot of pop-ups and fly balls.

What's Your Decision?

You are the manager.
The bases are loaded and you want a hit.
Which batter will you send to the plate?

#1 Zimmer

#2 Amoros

#3 Shuba

#4 Kellert

#5 Hoak

Choose the batter. Then turn the page to find out which batter the Dodgers' manager chose.

The Dodgers chose Shuba, #3.

Their reasons involved both offensive and defensive strategy. First of all, they wanted more runs. For that reason, they went with the percentages and brought in lefty Shuba to face the right-handed pitcher. Shuba's record as a pinch hitter showed that he had a good chance of hitting the ball solidly in this important situation. With runners in scoring position, Brooklyn needed a hitter who could make contact with the ball more than they needed Zimmer's power. A single was all that was needed to give Brooklyn a comfortable lead

The Dodgers were also thinking about defense. With a two-run lead and a good pitcher on the mound, they wanted their best defensive team on the field. It didn't matter if they went scoreless as long as the Yankees went scoreless as well. With Zimmer out of the game, Gilliam moved to second base, and Amoros came in at left field.

Here's What Happened!

Shuba grounded out and ended the Dodger threat. At the time, the strategy appeared to be a failure.

But in their next turn at bat, the Yankees put two men on base with none out. Left-handed power hitter Yogi Berra then stepped to the plate. Berra almost always pulled the ball to right field, so the Dodgers shifted their fielders to that side. But this happened to be a rare occasion when Berra sliced a pitch down the left-field foul line.

Amoros, who was playing about 100 feet off the line, had to sprint hard to try to reach the sinking liner. Both Yankee runners were sure that the ball would fall in for a hit, so they dashed around the bases. At the last instant, Amoros flung out his arm and made a stunning catch near the stands. The Yankee base runners screeched to a halt and tried to scramble back to their bases. Amoros quickly fired the ball back to the infield, and the Dodgers caught Gil McDougald before he could return to first base. It was a double play!

The Dodgers later agreed that Amoros was probably the only outfielder on the team who could have run down Berra's drive. Had he not caught the ball, two runs would have scored, and the Yankees would have had a man on second with no one out. Instead, no runs scored. New York never crossed the plate in the game and Brooklyn won, 2 to 0. Thanks to a minor defensive switch in their lineup, the Dodgers finally won a World Series.

Brooklyn's Sandy Amoros reaches out to make the catch that saved the Series for the Dodgers. His sixth-inning grab of a Yogi Berra drive choked off a Yankee rally and lifted the Bums to their first Series title.

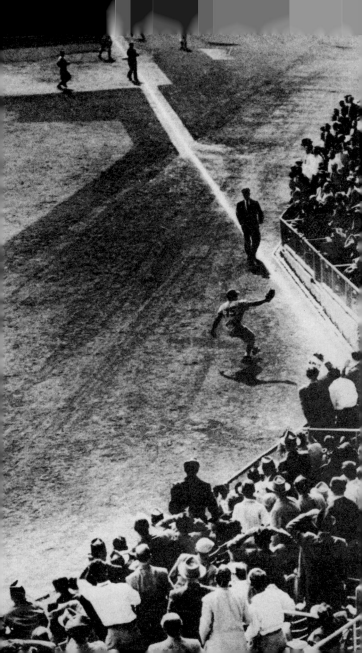

3 A Classic Choice: Hitting or Fielding

Who starts at shortstop?

A good glove...

Mark Belanger

...or a hot bat?

Kiko Garcia

You are managing
the Baltimore Orioles.

So far, this 1979 World Series against the Pittsburgh
Pirates has been everything you could ask for. With five
games played so far, you lead the Pirates three games
to two. Games six and seven (if needed) are to be
played in your friendly home park. Your managing,
especially your strategy in the fourth game, has drawn
rave reviews from commentators. When the Pirates
brought in Kent Tekulve, their ace right-handed relief
pitcher, you unleashed a series of left-handed pinch
hitters and blasted Pittsburgh out of the park.

As you approach game number six, however, you have
some worries. Some of your best hitters are no longer
doing the job, and your team's fielding has not been up to
your usual standards. This situation affects your decision
at shortstop, where you have two possible starters,
Kiko Garcia and Mark Belanger. Kiko averages one hit
every four at-bats, but is prone to defensive errors.
Belanger is not a good hitter but is a star infielder.
Which one will play?

	Batting Average	Home Runs	Fielding Errors
Garcia	.247	5	27
Belanger	.167	0	3

Belanger, at 35, is nine years older than Garcia. Although never a good hitter, he has been an All-Star shortstop during his career. He was forced to sit out a month earlier in the season with an injury that has since healed. During the play-offs, and so far in this Series, he has played true to form: one error, but only one hit.

Garcia, on the other hand, contributed a .273 average in the play-off series, but was also charged with 2 errors. In game number three of this Series, Garcia was the star batter. He collected four hits in that game, including a bases-loaded triple.

Consider the game's opposing pitchers.

Pittsburgh is going with left-handed John Candelaria. Although he did not have as fine a season as 1977, when he was 20-5, Candelaria's record of 14 wins and 9 losses was tops among Pirate hurlers. Pittsburgh has a flock of fine relievers, and it is not uncommon to see the team use four or five pitchers in a game. By changing pitchers frequently, Pittsburgh has limited the effectiveness of the Oriole pinch hitters.

Your pitcher will be hard-throwing Jim Palmer. Palmer has been named the American League's top pitcher in three different seasons and always seems to do well in crucial games. His throwing style includes a steady stream of high fastballs.

John Candelaria

Jim Palmer

Consider these other factors.

• Shortstop is judged to be one of the most important fielding positions because of the large number of grounders that are hit to that area.

• Two of your most powerful hitters, Eddie Murray and Lee May, are doing nothing to boost your offense. Murray, who hit .295 during the year with 25 home runs, is in a slump. He has done little more than fill up space in the batting order lately. Power hitter May is filling space on the bench. He is a poor fielder and is normally your designated hitter. But the DH rule is not used by National League teams and won't be allowed for this World Series. Therefore May is no longer in the regular lineup.

• You do have other hitters capable of providing scoring punch. Ken Singleton hit .295 with 35 homers this year, and Gary Roenicke, Doug DeCinces, and John Lowenstein combined for 52 home runs. But none of these players has been tearing up Pirate pitching.

In 1979, Gary Roenicke (left) blossomed into a fine young ball-player, smashing 25 home runs and hitting for a .261 average. Veteran switch hitter Ken Singleton had his finest year in 1979 also, knocking in 111 runs on the strength of 35 homers and a .295 batting average.

What's Your Decision?

You are the manager.
It's time to pencil in your lineup before the start of the game.
Who takes the field in the first inning?

#1 Garcia
#2 Belanger

Choose the player for shortstop. Then turn the page to find out which player the Orioles' manager chose.

The Orioles decided to start Garcia, #1.

Baltimore's manager had been impatient with the weak showing made by some of his offensive players. With Murray in a slump and May on the bench, the Orioles felt that they could not afford Belanger's weak hitting as well. Garcia, at least, had shown an ability to come up with a key hit in this Series. It was worth trying him again.

The decision might have been different if Palmer were a sinker-ball pitcher who caused batters to hit mainly grounders. But his high fastballs often resulted in more pop-ups and fly balls, so it was not as important for him to have a fine shortstop. Even if Garcia should happen to make an error, Palmer might be able to pitch the team's way out of trouble.

Here's What Happened!

Even with Garcia in the lineup, the Orioles were unable to get any runs off Candelaria in the first six innings. Fortunately, Palmer was throwing well, and he kept the game scoreless going into the seventh inning. But then the problems began.

Palmer retired the first batter, but then gave up a single to speedy outfielder Omar Moreno. Next, he got two quick strikes on Tim Foli and then got Foli to hit a bouncing ball up the middle. It seemed like an easy inning-ending double play until Palmer ticked the ball with his glove, slowing it down slightly. Garcia was practically standing on second base as both the ball and Moreno headed toward him. Kiko seemed to waver between charging the ball or waiting for it to get to him. In the end, he failed to field the ball cleanly. His indecision cost his team at least one out and possibly two, as both Moreno and Foli were safe.

It would have taken a great play by Garcia to have pulled off that double play, but Oriole fans had seen Belanger make great plays routinely.

Instead of retiring the side, Palmer now found himself facing runners on second and first, with only one out. With the help of another shaky fielding play by the Oriole second baseman, Pittsburgh went on to score twice in the inning. Candelaria and reliever Kent Tekulve shut out the Oriole batsmen, so two runs were all Pittsburgh needed to win the game. The Pirates went on to win the seventh game and became the 1979 World Series champions.

Next page: Keeping his foot on the base while fielding Tim Foli's grounder up the middle proved to be too much for Oriole shortstop Kiko Garcia. Pittsburgh's Omar Moreno slides safely into second on what could have been a double-play ball. Baltimore's fielding lapse opened the way for a Pirate rally and eventual win in game six.

4 A Fourth-Inning Trap

Tommy John's bat, idle for the past three seasons,
poses little threat to Los Angeles.

You are managing
the New York Yankees.

This 1981 World Series against the Los Angeles Dodgers presents you with more problems than you've faced all year. Because the American League allows a designated hitter for the pitcher and the National League does not, the Series is played using the designated hitter rule only every other year. This is the year that the designated hitter rule, under which you have played all season, is not in effect, so your pitchers have had to bat for themselves. This situation has forced you into an uncomfortable choice in the sixth game of the Series.

Trailing the Dodgers three games to two in the Series, you had selected veteran Tommy John as your starting pitcher. His opponent was the Dodgers' fine veteran Burt Hooton. A home run by Willie Randolph put you ahead 1 to 0 in the third inning, but the Dodgers came back to tie it up in the fourth.

In your half of the fourth inning, Larry Milbourne came to bat with a man on base and two outs. Los Angeles walked Milbourne, the eighth man in the batting order, knowing that this would bring Tommy John to the plate.

Tommy has never batted during the regular season. Aside from this Series, his last major league at-bat, in fact, was with the Dodgers in 1978. A .157 lifetime hitter, John has as much chance of getting a hit as your batboy does. But if you pull him now, you must replace him with another pitcher for the rest of the game. With two outs, two men on base, and the score tied in the fourth inning, do you pinch hit for John or do you let him bat?

Consider John's pitching performance.

The 38-year-old left-hander has been throwing his sinking pitches again this season with good effect. During the year, he won 9 games and lost 8, notching a fine 2.64 ERA. In game two of this Series, he stood up to the Dodgers by allowing no runs and only three hits in seven innings.

But in this game, John has not been quite as sharp as usual. In only four innings of work, he has already allowed six hits. He's been tough when it's counted, though, and the Dodgers have only one run to show for their six hits.

Look at the men warming up in your bullpen.

If you decide to send in a pinch hitter for John, you will have to come up with some strong pitching from your relievers. You have one of the game's finest relief men, Goose Gossage, but he is only effective during a couple of innings per game. Since it is only the fourth inning, you must look elsewhere for a pitcher who can carry you through at least the next two or three innings until you can put in Gossage.

Rich "Goose" Gossage's fastball has been clocked at 98 M.P.H. New York usually saves their fire-baller for the late innings, when his smoke is needed the most.

You have a number of middle-inning relievers whose 1981 season records were as follows:

	Wins-Losses	ERA	Saves
Ron Davis	4-5	2.71	6
George Frazier	0-1	1.61	3
Rudy May	6-11	4.14	1
Rick Reuschel*	8-11	3.10	0
Dave LaRoche	4-1	2.49	0

*Includes Reuschel's statistics with the Chicago Cubs before being traded to the Yankees in mid-season.

In postseason play, you have relied on the men who pitched the best at the end of the season, Davis and Frazier. The others have not received as much playing time lately and you cannot expect them to be at their sharpest. But it wouldn't take much from May, Reuschel, or LaRoche to match the World Series performances of Davis and Frazier so far. As their statistics show, these two men have not had an easy time getting outs against the Dodgers.

1981 World Series Records So Far

	Wins-Losses	Innings	Hits	ERA
Davis	0-0	2	3	13.50
Frazier	0-2	2²/₃	5	13.48

Davis has had control problems. Frazier lost both game three and game four as reliever.

George Frazier

Ron Davis

Now look at your possible pinch hitters.

Your team this year is so rich with talent that you have no shortage of good pinch hitters on the bench. Two of them in particular come to mind—Bobby Murcer and Lou Piniella.

Murcer had collected many key hits since he first saw regular action with the Yankees back in 1969. He has hit for both power and high average in his career, with lifetime bests of 33 homers and a .331 average. This left-handed hitter no longer swings the bat as well as he once did, but he still wound up the 1981 season with a .265 average.

Piniella also started his big-league career in 1969, when he was named the American League's Rookie of the Year. Lou swings from the right side of the plate and is one of the few players in baseball who has kept his lifetime batting average near .290. This past year he hit .277.

Steady Lou Piniella has batted around .290 in both regular season and postseason play throughout his career.

Bobby Murcer averages nearly twenty home runs a season. Still, he has never quite satisfied Yankee fans, who had expected him to be another Mickey Mantle.

Either John, Murcer, or Piniella will have to face Burt Hooton, a right-hander who has enjoyed a great season. Burt won 11 games and lost 6 during the year, with a sparkling 2.28 ERA.

What's Your Decision?

You are the manager.
Your team has frustrated you by leaving base runners stranded at a record rate for a World Series.
Who will bat for you?

#1 Will you let John bat and give up this chance to score?

#2 Will you pinch hit for John and hope for a good performance from an unreliable bullpen?

Choose between John and a pinch hitter. Then turn the page to find out what choice the Yankees' manager made.

The Yankees decided on choice #2.

Their manager decided to go for the runs to break the game open. Murcer was called in to bat against Hooton. Meanwhile, Frazier and Davis were warming up quickly. It would be left to them to hold on until it was time for Gossage to get into the game.

Here's What Happened!

Murcer lined a pitch deep to right field but it was caught for the third out of the inning. Again the Yankees had wasted a pair of base runners.

With John out of the game, Frazier came in to pitch and was greeted by a long string of hard-hitting Dodgers. Los Angeles, relieved to see that John was out of the game, pounded Frazier for four hits and three runs in the fifth inning.

Ron Davis came in in the sixth inning. His sidearm fastballs continued to miss the mark. Davis retired only one batter while giving up two walks and a hit, so he was replaced by Rick Reuschel. By the time Reuschel finally put a stop to the Dodger rally, New York found themselves trailing 8 to 1!

It was the nearly unanimous opinion of onlookers that the Yankees should have left John in the game. Following that error in strategy, New York never had a chance, and they lost, 9 to 2. Los Angeles took the championship, 4 games to 2.

Tommy John, angry after being lifted for a pinch hitter in the fourth, tries to remain calm in the Yankee dugout.

5 First Base Is Open

San Francisco's Jack Sanford and New York's Ralph Terry square off one last time in game seven of the 1962 World Series.

You are managing
the New York Yankees.

It's 1962, and, as usual, your team is in the World Series. A tough San Francisco Giants team has battled you into the seventh and final game.

Each team boasts an ace starting pitcher. Jack Sanford is pitching for San Francisco, and Ralph Terry is leading your Yankees. These two have dueled each other twice already in thrilling games, with Sanford winning game two of the Series 2 to 0 and Terry winning game five, 5 to 3.

Once again these right-handers have been at it, each mowing down the opposition in this deciding game. After four scoreless innings, your team finally broke through for a run. As the game went on, your batters had plenty of chances to widen the lead. But the Giants wriggled out of two bases-loaded jams without allowing you another score. As the game went into the ninth inning, you led 1 to 0.

But now Terry has run into trouble. Leading off the ninth inning, Matty Alou beat out a bunt for a base hit. Terry came back and struck out both Felipe Alou and Chuck Hiller. Just one out away from victory, Terry then watched Willie Mays drill one of his pitches to deep right field for a double. Only a quick recovery by right fielder Roger Maris kept Alou from scoring the tying run.

Now there are runners on second and third, with slugger Willie McCovey coming to the plate. First base is open and you only need one more out. Do you pitch to McCovey, or walk him?

Take a look at the next two Giant batters.

Young Willie McCovey, although not a full-time starter, is a dangerous hitter. This 6-foot, 4-inch, 210-pound first baseman blasted 20 home runs in only 229 times at bat this season. If he had played full time, McCovey would have led the majors with 50 homers at that rate. McCovey's .293 average shows more than just raw power. So far in the Series, he has had 3 hits in 14 trips to the plate.

Since right-handed pitchers prefer to pitch to right-handed batters, you could walk left-handed McCovey. Then right-hander Terry would be facing the right-handed hitter Orlando Cepeda. Cepeda, however, is even more firmly established as a star slugger than McCovey. Orlando has enjoyed an All-Star season with a .306 average and 35 home runs.

Orlando Cepeda (top), and Willie McCovey (bottom) both enjoyed fine seasons with the Giants. Neither would be a pushover for Ralph Terry in the ninth.

Cepeda, though, has always had trouble against American League pitchers. He didn't get his first hit of the Series until game six, and his totals for the Series games so far read: 3 hits in 19 times at bat for a .158 average, no home runs.

Now consider your pitching staff.

Once before in World Series play, Terry was in an almost identical situation and the result was disaster. Two years earlier he had taken the mound in the ninth inning of the final game of the championship against the Pittsburgh Pirates. With the score tied at 9 to 9, Terry had pitched to right-handed hitter Bill Mazeroski, who hit the home run that gave Pittsburgh the title.

Ralph is a better pitcher now than he was in 1960, when he was just breaking into the Yankees' pitching rotation. This past year he posted a 23-12 record and a fine 3.19 ERA. In nearly three complete games during this Series, he has given up only 5 runs. Terry's record against McCovey, however, is not perfect. Willie clouted a home run off him in game number two.

Your top relief specialist is Marshall Bridges. A left-hander, Bridges won 8 and lost 4 in 1962, with 18 saves and an ERA of 3.14. In 3⅔ innings of World Series work, he has allowed San Francisco two runs.

Marshall Bridges has had his best year in baseball in 1962, finishing second in saves among American League pitchers. The grand slam he fed up to Chuck Hiller in game four of the Series, though, broke that game open for the Giants.

What's Your Decision?

You are the manager.
You must prevent the Giants from scoring the tying run.
How will you handle McCovey?

#1 Will you let Terry pitch to McCovey?

#2 Will you have Terry walk McCovey and pitch to Cepeda?

#3 Will you bring in the left-handed Bridges to pitch to McCovey?

Choose the strategy. Then turn the page to find out which strategy the Yankees' manager chose.

The Yankees decided on #1.

They stayed with their big winner, Terry, and gave him a chance to redeem himself for the 1960 loss. Terry told his manager that he would like to take his chances pitching to McCovey, instead of walking him to get to the more experienced Cepeda. The manager agreed.

Here's What Happened!

McCovey ripped one of Terry's pitches but had to watch as it curved into foul territory for strike one. Even after seeing Willie make such solid contact, the Yankees refused to change strategies. Terry continued to throw to McCovey, who found another pitch to his liking and drilled a line shot to the right of second base. That happened to be the exact spot where Yankee second baseman Bobby Richardson was positioned. Richardson did not have to move a step as he snared the high liner for the final out. Terry and the Yankees were champions.

Since the strategy produced the final out and a World Series win, it would have to be called successful. But if McCovey's drive had happened to sail only a foot higher, the result would have been different. Then Yankee fans would have had all winter to question why, with first base open, McCovey had not been walked.

6 The Fourth Outfielder

Who will be left out?

Al Kaline   Jim Northrup   Willie Horton   Mickey Stanley

You are managing the Detroit Tigers.

It's 1968, and for the first time in 23 years, your team has won the American League pennant. You now look forward to facing the St. Louis Cardinals in a battle for the World Series title.

One of the players most affected by this long dry spell was your great right fielder Al Kaline. Al put in 16 brilliant seasons as an all-around star before finally being on a pennant-winning team. Al's bad luck seems to have continued, however, because he was sidelined with injuries for much of this championship season.

In Al's absence, the rest of the Tiger outfield has played well. Kaline now seems to be fairly healthy, but you hate to break up an effective and winning combination in the outfield. Should you try to get Kaline back into the lineup for the Series, or should you leave well enough alone?

Consider each of your outfielders.

Right fielder Jim Northrup is a steady all-around player who can field and hit well. During the season, Northrup batted .264 with 21 home runs.

Left field has belonged to Willie Horton, a muscular power hitter. His 36 home runs and .285 average more than make up for the fact that he is the weakest of your fielders.

Center fielder Mickey Stanley can't match the others with his hitting. This season he hit for a modest .259 average with 11 home runs. But the fleet Tiger is considered one of the top defensive outfielders in the game. He has reached flies that most outfielders could not have reached and has relied on his quick hands and strong, accurate arm to get him through the entire season without making a single error!

Kaline is, without a doubt, a future Hall of Fame player. He has been able to do everything well on the baseball field, whether it has been hitting, fielding, throwing, or base running. Even in limited action this year he has contributed 10 homers and a .287 average. Throughout most of his career, he has been good for at least a .300 average and 20-30 home runs a season.

One of the all-time Tiger greats, Al Kaline has worn a Detroit uniform for 16 seasons and has yet to play in the World Series.

Having spent most of his 16th season on the injured list, though, Al may have trouble regaining his old form. In fact, he may actually be at the end of his effective career. Obviously, you would like to see a great player like Kaline finally get a chance to play in a World Series. But is it fair to take such a chance just for sentimental reasons?

This is the outfield that helped the Tigers win the American League pennant by 12 games and contributed to Detroit's league-leading 185 home runs: Jim Northrup (opposite page), Willie Horton (top), and Mickey Stanley.

Consider the rest of your team.

Your infield consists of good gloves and weak bats. Of the four starting infielders, only first baseman Norm Cash has hit with any consistency. None of the others even topped .250. Don Wert managed only .200 playing at third base, and shortstop Ray Oyler hit a terrible .135. They have done well, however, at manning these important fielding positions, and the outfielders have hit so well that your infielders' poor hitting did not hurt your season.

Late in the year, you experimented with Mickey Stanley at shortstop. He had never played shortstop before, and you know it would be a huge risk to have him play there in the Series. Besides, you would miss his tremendous fielding in center field.

This has been the "Year of the Pitcher." Pitchers so dominated batters that only one batter in the American League topped .300. Things were no different in the National League, where St. Louis' Bob Gibson recorded an unbelievable 1.12 ERA. You will need all the batting power you can get against Gibson and company in the Series. But you also realize that a single Tiger error may allow St. Louis to score the only run Gibson needs to win his game. With all these facts in mind, what will you do with your aging star, Kaline?

What's Your Decision?

You are the manager.
You have four good players for three positions.
Who will you put in to start the Series?

#1 Will you keep your winning outfield the way it is and leave Kaline on the bench?

#2 Will you play Kaline in place of Horton? Stanley? Northrup?

#3 Will you make room for Kaline by risking Stanley at shortstop?

#4 Will you include Kaline by rotating the outfielders each game?

Choose the lineup. Then turn the page to find out which lineup the Tigers' manager chose.

The Tigers selected option #3.

Baseball experts were shocked when, for the World Series, Kaline moved to right field, Northrup to center, and Stanley to shortstop. The move weakened Detroit's defense in two positions. Obviously the inexperienced Stanley could not hope to handle shortstop the way Oyler could. Nor could Northrup, now in center field, cover ground the way Stanley could.

Detroit was willing to take the risk. Because they wanted their best players in the lineup, and since four of their best players were outfielders, a new position had to be found for one of them. They felt that Stanley's natural defensive skill would allow him to catch on to the shortstop position enough so that he wouldn't make any serious errors.

Here's What Happened!

The changes did nothing to help the Tigers at first, and they fell behind the Cardinals three games to one. That meant that the Cards needed to win only one of the last three games to be champions and, if all else failed, they were sure they could count on Gibson to win game seven.

But Kaline's bat came in handy in game five as he cracked a bases-loaded single in the seventh inning to spark a Tiger win. Northrup's grand-slam home run in game six then helped Detroit to even the Series. Finally in the deciding game Northrup clouted a triple off Gibson, winning the title for his team.

Although Stanley and Northrup each made two errors in the Series, none of them was critical. Kaline, meanwhile, batted .379 for the Series with 2 homers and 8 runs batted in (RBIs). Northrup hit .250 with 2 home runs and 8 timely RBIs, while Horton added a .304 average and a home run. Stanley hit only .214, but even that was 79 points higher than Oyler's season average. With the help of good pitching, luck, and fine play by the four outfielders, the Tigers got away with their chancy move.

Jim Northrup cracks a two-run triple off Cardinal ace Bob Gibson in the seventh inning of game seven. The two runs were all Detroit needed to beat Gibson, who before this game had set a record by winning seven Series games in a row.

7 Any Place for Tenace?

Pete Rose displays Cincinnati's aggressive style of base-running as he charges from first to third on a single.

You are managing the Oakland A's.

Your team is the underdog in the 1972 World Series against the powerful Cincinnati Reds. An injury to your star slugger, Reggie Jackson, has left you with a struggling offense that reminds many onlookers of the famous "Hitless Wonders" of 1906. (A Chicago White Sox team earned that nickname by winning the pennant despite a team batting average of only .230.) Only the shocking batting success of reserve catcher Gene Tenace has kept your team from being wiped out by the Reds.

Unfortunately, Tenace's hot hitting has been accompanied by his defensive weakness. The Reds have been getting more daring on the base paths and Tenace has been unable to throw them out.

This is the seventh and final game of the Series. You want to keep Tenace in the game for his offense, but you are afraid that the Reds' base-stealing will give them an advantage. How are you going to solve this problem?

You know that the Reds have a history of swiping bases.

This season, Joe Morgan and Bobby Tolan have been the main culprits. Morgan stole 58 bases during the year, ranking second in the National League, while Tolan rated fifth with 42. Tolan has found Tenace to be an especially easy mark in the Series and so far has stolen four bases on him.

Joe Morgan

Bobby Tolan

In fact, Cincinnati's runners might as well have had a police escort protecting their base running. In the last five games, the Reds have stolen 11 bases and forced a throwing error. Only once has a Cincinnati player been thrown out attempting to steal.

Much of the blame for the Reds' stealing success lies with your starting pitchers. They were supposed to pitch carefully to keep the Reds from leading off too far, but they have failed to do so. Your starting pitcher in this game, however, is John "Blue Moon" Odom. Unlike the other starters on your team, Odom does well at holding base runners close to the bag.

John Odom

Consider the possibilities for juggling your lineup.

Dave Duncan was your regular catcher for most of the year, and there is no doubt that he has better defensive skills than Tenace. Unfortunately, Duncan carries around a featherweight batting average of .218.

Actually, Tenace did not hit much better during the regular season, batting only .225 with five home runs. But suddenly he seems to have convinced himself that he is the next Babe Ruth. He has swatted four homers in the first six games of the Series, batting over .300 while the rest of the A's struggle to hit .200.

Tenace has seen action during the year at positions other than catcher. Gene appeared in 49 games as catcher, 9 as outfielder, 7 as first baseman, and even played a handful of games at other infield positions. Because he is a fairly slow runner, though, he has not really mastered the art of playing defense at any position.

Though Gene Tenace's hitting in the Series has been sensational, his inability to hold the lid on Cincinnati's base stealers is causing Oakland concern. Would Dave Duncan do a better job in stopping the Reds' larceny?

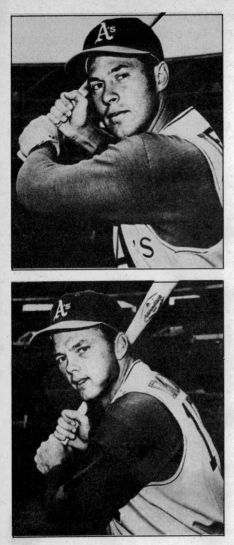

Gene Tenace

Dave Duncan

Two of your regulars, Matty Alou and Mike Epstein, have suffered through a miserable World Series so far. Alou has managed only one hit in the six games. This is highly unusual for Matty, who has been one of baseball's top singles hitters for a decade. In 1968, he came within a lucky bounce or two of beating Pete Rose for a batting title. During the past season, he has notched a .307 average.

For all the good he has done with it in the Series, Mike Epstein (0 for 16) might have been better off keeping his bat on his shoulder.

Big first baseman Epstein has done even worse and is still looking for his first World Series hit. Like Alou, Epstein is a proven hitter whose poor showing is a mystery. During the regular season, he hit .270 and led the club with 26 home runs. The weak-swinging A's could use his power.

What's Your Decision?

You are the manager.
You must put together a lineup that's sharp at both offense and defense.
Who will play, and where?

#1 Will you leave Tenace in as catcher and rely on pitcher Odom to keep the Reds from running?

#2 Will you replace Tenace behind the plate with Duncan, figuring that defense is more important and that Tenace's luck is due to run out?

#3 Will you let Duncan catch and put Tenace on first base in place of Epstein?

#4 Will you let Duncan catch and have Tenace take over for Alou in the outfield?

Choose the lineup. Then turn the page to find out which lineup the A's manager chose.

The A's went for choice #3.

With Duncan behind the plate and Odom on the mound, the A's would be well prepared to stop the Reds' running. But Tenace had been hitting so well that the manager felt it would be foolish to leave him on the bench, especially when the A's were having trouble getting runs.

The two positions where Tenace's slow defense would hurt the least were in the outfield and at first base. Since Tenace has neither speed nor an exceptional arm, he would probably do better at first base, where neither is very important. This meant that slugger Epstein, who normally hits much better than Tenace, would be out of the game. But the A's reasoned that, in a short series, it would be foolish to replace a hot hitter with a struggling one, no matter what their past records indicated.

Here's What Happened!

Tenace wasted no time in showing that he was still in the hitting groove. He singled in the first inning, bringing home the game's first run.

Oakland held on to that lead until the fourth inning, when Joe Morgan drew a walk off Odom. By throwing to first several times before he pitched, Odom held Morgan close to the base and nearly picked him off. When Blue Moon finally did throw to the plate, Morgan dashed off to steal second base. But Duncan's throw beat Morgan to the bag by the width of a shoelace, and the base runner was called out. Instead of having a man in scoring position with one out, there were two outs and no one on base. A possible rally had been stopped.

In the sixth inning, Tenace blasted a double that led to two more Oakland runs. The A's held on to their lead and won the game, 3 to 2, taking the Series. Gene Tenace had figured in all three Oakland runs, and Dave Duncan had stamped out a possible big inning for the Reds. Rarely had a baseball strategy worked so well!

Gene Tenace shows the batting form that won him World Series Most Valuable Player honors. Tenace tied a Series record with four home runs, knocked in nine of Oakland's sixteen runs, and hit .348, compared to the A's team batting average of .209.

Big Bob Robertson likes to use his muscles to swing for the fences, which he reached 26 times during the 1971 season.

You are managing
the Pittsburgh Pirates.

It's World Series time in 1971, but so far only your opponents, the Baltimore Orioles, have done any real playing. Baltimore won the first two games so easily that some fans are wondering if your Pirates have any business challenging them for the title.

Game number three, however, has finally provided some suspense. An excellent showing from your pitcher Steve Blass has held the Oriole hitters in check. You now lead 2 to 1 in the bottom of the seventh inning.

Roberto Clemente, the only hitter on your team who has worried the Orioles so far, opened the inning by bouncing to Oriole pitcher Mike Cuellar. But Cuellar threw wild to first base and Clemente was safe. Cuellar then made another mistake by walking the slumping Willie Stargell. With two on and no one out, first baseman Bob Robertson is next at bat. This is a good time for a sacrifice bunt to move the runners to scoring position. But do you really want Robertson to bunt?

Look at the Orioles to see if a bunt would be favorable.

It is obvious that the Orioles do not expect a bunt. They know that the Pirates, especially Robertson, have a reputation as a free-swinging group of hitters. Baltimore's third baseman, Brooks Robinson, is playing very deep at third base, expecting Robertson to take a full swing. Brooks may be the finest fielder in all of baseball.

Mike Cuellar, Baltimore's pitcher, is a veteran who has won at least 20 games in each of the past three seasons. This season he sported a fine 3.08 ERA, proving that it isn't easy to score off him. Ordinarily, a left-hander like Cuellar would be considered at a disadvantage against Robertson, a right-handed hitter. But Mike has a weird assortment of screwballs and other pitches that actually make him at least as tough on a right-hander as on a lefty. As fine a pitcher as Cuellar is, however, you can't help but wonder whether he still has his confidence after making two mistakes in a row.

Neither all-time great third baseman Brooks Robinson (left), MVP of the 1970 Series, nor Mike Cuellar, the left-handed Cuban with the nasty screwball, expects Pirate slugger Robertson to bunt.

Now consider Robertson
and the other players on your team.

Robertson is probably the last person you would want batting in a bunting situation. No one on your bench can even remember if he has bunted at all this season. At over 6 feet tall and 195 pounds, Robertson is known for his power rather than for his bat control.

Bob has proven to be a tough out this season, his second full one in the majors. He slugged 26 home runs and batted .271 during the regular season. Then, in the play-off series against San Francisco, he pounded rival pitchers for four home runs to spark the Pirate win.

Baltimore had won 16 games in a row, including two in this Series, before facing Steve Blass in game three. Blass won 15 games in 1971 and shared the National League lead with five shutouts. This game marked his first World Series appearance ever.

Catcher Manny Sanguillen bats after Robertson. An excellent hitter, Manny hit .319 during the season. If Robertson moves the runners along with a sacrifice, Baltimore may walk Sanguillen to set up a force play at home.

Your team is in a deep batting slump. In the first two games, they collected only 11 hits, a good share of those belonging to Clemente. Based on what your players have done so far in the Series, it is doubtful that they can come up with a big inning.

Both Roberto Clemente (left), a .317 lifetime hitter, and Manny Sanguillen, who led all National League catchers in batting with a .319 average in 1971, must hit well if Pittsburgh is to take the Championship from Baltimore, last year's World Series winners.

Robertson is now looking at your third base coach to see if there are any special instructions for him on this pitch. The base runners are also waiting to see if you have anything to signal to them.

What's Your Decision?

You are the manager.
The pitcher is ready to throw.
What will your signal be?

#1 Will you send in the bunt order?
#2 Will you let Robertson hit away?

Choose the signal. Then turn the page to find out which signal the Pirates' manager gave.

The Pirates chose #1, the bunt.

The fact that Brooks Robinson was playing back so far at third base convinced the Pirates to let Robertson try to move up the runners. Given that much room, they reasoned, even a poor bunter like Bob should be able to do the job.

The Pirates were also having trouble with offense, and they chose to play for one or two runs rather than depend on their free swingers to produce a big inning. With a one-run lead and a steady pitcher going for them, Pittsburgh felt they could afford to play this way. Had they been five runs behind, they would have had to try for a big rally and would not have wanted to sacrifice an out.

Here's What Happened!

The bunt signal surprised some of the Pirates so much that Clemente, the runner on second base, tried to call a time out to make sure the signal was correct. But Cuellar went into his wind-up and threw his screwball to the plate before time could be called.

As it turned out, Robertson had not been paying close enough attention to his coaches and had missed the bunt sign altogether! This was dangerous because the Pirate runners, who were expecting a bunt, would be poised to run the instant the ball reached the plate. If Robertson failed to bunt or if he hit the ball in the air, they could easily be caught off base. Fortunately, the big first baseman hit the pitch so solidly that it sailed over the fence for a home run.

By ignoring his manager's strategy, Robertson gave his team a 5 to 1 lead and put the game out of Baltimore's reach. Never has a manager been so happy to see his decision proven wrong!

This game put Pittsburgh behind in the Series by only one game and was the beginning of their turnaround. Pittsburgh went on to win the Series.

Bob Robertson missed his coach's bunt sign, but got all of Mike Cuellar's delivery, connecting for a game-breaking home run.

9

Seventh Game Dilemma: Drysdale or Koufax

The pitching combination of Sandy Koufax (left) and Don Drysdale has secured the Dodgers a place in the 1965 World Series.

You are managing
the Los Angeles Dodgers.

Your team is about to face the Minnesota Twins for the seventh game of the 1965 World Series. This year's Dodger team has been blessed with tremendous pitching skill, which has made up for some rather unimpressive hitting. Who will be the starting pitcher in this deciding game? Will you start Don Drysdale, or Sandy Koufax?

Either Drysdale or Koufax would be an excellent choice. You consider Koufax to be the best pitcher in baseball and Drysdale to be just a notch below him. But while right-hander Drysdale has had three days of rest since his last game, Koufax has had only two.

Most managers would love to have the problem that you now face, but that doesn't make your decision any easier. Who gets the starting assignment?

You study the Twins' lineup to see which pitcher would be most effective.

The Twins seem to have put together a powerful, well-balanced batting order. They sport some high batting averages and big home run totals from both sides of the plate. During the 1965 season, their top hitters earned the following marks:

Right-handed Batters

	Average	Home Runs
Killebrew	.269	25
Allison	.233	23
Versalles	.273	19
Battey	.297	6

Left-handed Batters

	Average	Home Runs
Oliva	.321	16
Mincher	.251	22
Hall	.285	20
Valdespino	.261	1

In game four of this Series, mild-mannered Harmon Killebrew belted a round-tripper off Drysdale.

Harmon Killebrew is firmly established as the American League's top home run hitter, but his totals are lower this year as a result of a pulled hamstring which put him out for part of the season. Bob Allison, who normally hits for a higher average, has been in a slump. Things have gotten no better for him in the World Series, where he has been striking out regularly. Zoilo Versalles, the speedy shortstop, was voted the American League's Most Valuable Player for the season.

As for the left-handed hitters, Tony Oliva topped the American League in batting average for the second year in a row, Don Mincher has been a reserve most of his career, but he hit so well while filling in for the injured Killebrew that he has remained in the lineup. After a fine start, Jimmie Hall has tailed off somewhat, though not nearly as badly as Allison has.

You now look at the records of your pitchers.

1965 Season

	Wins-Losses	ERA	Shutouts	Strikeouts
Koufax	26-8	2.04	8	382 (Record)
Drysdale	23-12	2.77	7	210

Both men lost their first World Series start this year but came back to win their second. Drysdale has been hit harder than Koufax. He has allowed over three runs per game during the Series, while Koufax has an ERA closer to one.

Drysdale is especially effective against right-handed batters because his sidearm delivery makes it look as if the ball is aimed right at them. Koufax throws more overhand and can be equally effective against right-handed and left-handed batters.

Don is also one of those rare pitchers who poses a real threat when it is his turn to bat. During the season, he hit .300, and his seven home runs tied a league record for pitchers! He is much more likely to help your team score runs than is Koufax, who batted only .177.

Koufax has been bothered by arm troubles which the doctors tell him are incurable. He is usually in pain between starts and rarely throws at all during the three days' rest he normally gets between outings. His tender arm also means that he must take more time warming up than Drysdale.

Since this is the last game of the year, there is no reason why you could not use both pitchers if the starter should get in trouble. You also have an expert reliever, left-hander Ron Perranoski, ready for action.

What's Your Decision?

> You are the manager.
> You must inform one of these pitchers that he will start.
> **Who will take the mound for your Dodgers?**
>
> **#1** Sandy Koufax
> **#2** Don Drysdale

Choose the pitcher. Then turn the page to find out which pitcher the Dodgers' manager chose.

The Dodgers called on Koufax, #1.

Los Angeles manager Walt Alston called this the most difficult decision he had ever faced in baseball. But as good a pitcher as Drysdale was, Koufax was simply awesome in 1965. The Dodgers gambled that, just this once, Sandy's arm could take the strain of pitching without his usual three days of rest.

There were two other reasons why Koufax was chosen. First, Drysdale would be the better choice as a reliever. If Koufax ran into problems as the starter, the Dodgers would have both right-handed Drysdale and lefty Perranoski in reserve. But if Drysdale started and was hit hard, Los Angeles would be left without a right-handed ace in the bullpen. Drysdale's healthier arm also made him a better choice for handling the short warm-up time that relief pitchers often have to cope with.

Secondly, with Allison struggling at the plate, the Dodgers feared the Twins' left-handed lineup more than they did the right-handed one. They would prefer to use their left-hander to stop Oliva, Mincher, and the others.

Here's What Happened!

Koufax pitched one of his typically marvelous games. His fastball handcuffed the Minnesota batters, who managed only three hits off him. Koufax shut out the Twins 2 to 0, winning the final game of the Series.

Sandy blanked the Twins on three hits, while striking out ten to raise his Series total to 29 in three games. Here he rears back to fire against the American League's top hitter, Tony Oliva.

10 Gator Aid: Sparky or the Goose?

Who can replace Ron Guidry, known to his teammates as Gator, to save the game?

You are managing
the New York Yankees.

This 1978 season has been a strange one. When you took over as manager in midyear, the Yankees were 14 games behind the Boston Red Sox and fading fast. But then, just as the Red Sox fell apart, your team somehow regrouped. You ended the season tied with the Red Sox for first place in the American League's Eastern Division. The entire 162-game season has boiled down to this one final play-off game to determine the divisional champ.

Your ace pitcher, Ron Guidry, also known as "Louisiana Lightning" and "Gator," threw well before tiring in the seventh inning. When he left the game, you owned a 4 to 2 lead at Boston's Fenway Park. Rich "Goose" Gossage came in to protect that lead, and the Yankees added to it with a run in the top of the eighth. Considering Gossage's awesome fastball, that lead should have been safe. But the Red Sox have one of baseball's toughest batting orders, and in the eighth inning they began to drill Gossage's pitches.

Jerry Remy led off the inning for Boston with a double. Jim Rice was retired, but then Carl Yastrzemski singled, allowing Remy to score. Carlton Fisk added a single. Fred Lynn whacked yet another hit and Yastrzemski scored. Suddenly your lead has dwindled to 5-4 with two Red Sox runners on base and still only one out.

Sparky Lyle has been warming up in your bullpen. Is it time to pull Gossage out of the game and put in Lyle?

Some of the facts favor staying with Gossage.

Goose has been your main relief pitcher this season and has produced better statistics than Lyle:

	Wins-Losses	ERA	Saves
Gossage	10-11	2.01	27
Lyle	9-3	3.47	9

Gossage has been particularly strong over the last half of the year and has averaged almost one strikeout per inning. At 27 years of age, he has just entered his prime as a pitcher. Lyle is 34 years old and, in your opinion, seems to be slipping just a bit. Sparky has made no secret of the fact that he is upset by being demoted to number-two reliever.

Goose Gossage led the American League with 27 saves in 1978. Yet even Gossage is having trouble dousing Boston's explosive attack.

Despite his young age, Gossage is a proven veteran. In 1975, while he was with the White Sox, he won an award as the American League's top reliever. Two years later, as an All-Star performer for the Pittsburgh Pirates, he struck out 151 batters in 133 innings.

The next two Red Sox batters are right-handed hitters who have not had the best of seasons. Butch Hobson, who hit .250 with 17 home runs during the year, is due up next. He is followed by George Scott, who hit .233 with 12 homers. Gossage, who throws right-handed, has an advantage against these men over left-handed Lyle.

Other facts, however, lean in Lyle's favor.

Over the past five years, Lyle has baffled at least as many batters as Gossage has. In 1977, in fact, Sparky chalked up 13 wins, 26 saves, and a 2.17 ERA. With these impressive totals, he won the American League's Cy Young Award as its top pitcher. That was only a year ago. Could Lyle have suddenly lost all his skill in so short a time?

As good as Gossage may be, this doesn't seem to be his day. Four of the last five batters have hit safely against him. If he allows one more hit, your whole season is in grave danger.

Veteran relief specialist Sparky Lyle, who started his career with Boston, has saved twenty or more games in five previous seasons.

Sometimes players perform differently when the pressure gets fierce than they do under normal circumstances. Perhaps part of Goose's problem today is that this is the first postseason game he has pitched in his life. Lyle, on the other hand, has proven that he can bear down harder in tense play-off games. He has won three and lost none in postseason play during his career, allowing only two runs in more than 17 innings of work.

What's Your Decision?

You are the manager.
Boston's Hobson is now digging in at the plate and the Red Sox runners are preparing to take their leads from the bases.
Who will pitch for you?

#1 Will you stay with Gossage?
#2 Will you bring in Lyle?

Choose the pitcher. Then turn the page to find out which pitcher the Yankees' manager chose.

The Yankees stayed with Gossage, #1.

Things might have been different if the struggling Gossage had been faced with two tough left-handed batters such as Lynn and Yastrzemski. But with two right-handers due up, both of whom were having problems hitting, New York felt that right-handed Gossage could control the situation.

Here's What Happened!

Gossage threw nothing but fastballs and easily retired both Hobson and Scott. New York escaped the inning with a one-run lead.

But the problem was far from over! In the ninth inning, Gossage returned to the mound and retired the first batter, Dwight Evans. But then he walked Rick Burleson. Remy then hit a line drive to right field that should have been caught by Lou Piniella. Right fielder Piniella, however, lost the ball in the sun and it fell in for a hit. Fortunately for New York, Burleson had hesitated before running the bases and had been forced to stop at second. Rice then hit a long fly ball that would have scored Burleson had he gotten to third on the previous play.

Now there are two outs, two men on base, and left-hander Carl Yastrzemski is scheduled to bat with Lynn to follow. Will you stay with Gossage? Again you must decide whether to keep Gossage or replace him with Lyle.

Normally a dependable outfielder, Lou Piniella couldn't quite reach this high drive to right field.

Two new factors enter into this decision.

Gossage has looked stronger this inning. In fact, the game should really be over, as Remy's drive was a catchable ball.

But the last four left-handed hitters for Boston have all hit safely off Gossage. Lefty Yastrzemski is a dangerous clutch hitter with 18 years of experience in the majors. This past season he hit .277 with 17 homers.

Carl Yastrzemski is a three-time winner of the American League's batting title and the 1967 winner of the Triple Crown and MVP award. Before coming to bat with the winning run on base in the ninth inning, Yaz homered off Guidry in the second.

The famous Yaz swing.

What's Your Decision?

You are the manager.
Who pitches now?

#1 Gossage
#2 Lyle

Again choose the pitcher. Then turn the page to find out which pitcher the Yankees' manager chose this time.

The Yankees again stayed with Gossage, #1.

Instead of playing the percentages this time, New York decided to win or lose the pennant with the man they believed to be their best pitcher. They didn't want to trust Lyle, whom they saw as aging and angry.

Here's What Happened!

New York's strategy again paid off as Yastrzemski popped up to end the game and give New York the title. The decision shocked Lyle and many of his teammates, and had it backfired there would have been mutterings about the move all winter long. But Goose Gossage and his fastball were good enough to make the strategy pay off.

The Yankees win the pennant!

YOU CAN MATCH WITS WITH PROFESSIONAL LEAGUE COACHES

★ YOU ARE THE COACH SERIES ★

by Nate Aaseng

Using statistics from actually played games, sports fans will be asked to make crucial decisions for major league teams. The actual coaching decisions and the game results are revealed at the end of each book so readers can rate themselves against the pros.

LAUREL-LEAF BOOKS

So, *Play Ball* with:

____ YOU ARE THE COACH:
   FOOTBALL ....(99136-6)

____ YOU ARE THE COACH:
   BASKETBALL ....(99128-5)

____ YOU ARE THE COACH:
   HOCKEY ....(99843-3)

____ YOU ARE THE MANAGER:
   BASEBALL...(99829-8)

$1.95 each

At your local bookstore or use this handy coupon for ordering:

Dell DELL BOOKS
P.O. BOX 1000, PINE BROOK, N.J. 07058-1000   B118A

Please send me the books I have checked above. I am enclosing S _____ (please add 75c per copy to cover postage and handling). Send check or money order—no cash or C.O.D.'s. Please allow up to 8 weeks for shipment.

Name _____

Address _____

City_____ State/Zip _____